SPORTS IN ACTION

SKATEBOARDING in Action

John Crossingham

Photographs by Marc Crabtree

Illustrations by Bonna Rouse

 Crabtree Publishing Company

www.crabtreebooks.com

Created by Bobbie Kalman

Dedicated by John Crossingham
For Chris Mills, who makes a mean tea

Editor-in-Chief
Bobbie Kalman

Author
John Crossingham

Project editor
Amanda Bishop

Editors
Niki Walker
Kathryn Smithyman

Copy editor
Jaimie Nathan

Cover and title page design
Campbell Creative Services

Computer design
Margaret Amy Reiach

Production coordinator
Heather Fitzpatrick

Photo research
Heather Fitzpatrick
Jaimie Nathan

Consultant
Dallas Green

Special thanks to
Mike Carr, Mike Armstrong, Ryan Brown,
Phil Shore, and Shred Central Skatepark

Photographs
Marc Crabtree: front cover, back cover, pages 5,
6, 10, 12-15, 17, 20, 21-25, 26 (bottom), 27, 28, 31
Other images by Corbis Images and Digital Stock

Illustrations
All illustrations by Bonna Rouse except
the following:
Margaret Amy Reiach: border, chapter heading
Trevor Morgan: page 6

Crabtree Publishing Company

www.crabtreebooks.com   1-800-387-7650

PMB 16A
350 Fifth Avenue
Suite 3308
New York, NY
10118

612 Welland Avenue
St. Catharines
Ontario
Canada
L2M 5V6

73 Lime Walk
Headington
Oxford
OX3 7AD
United Kingdom

Cataloging-in-Publication Data
Crossingham, John
 Skateboarding in action / John Crossingham;
illustrations by Bonna Rouse.
    p. cm. -- (Sports in action)
Includes index.
This book outlines the equipment, techniques, skills, and
competitions common to the sport of skateboarding.
  ISBN 0-7787-0117-4 (RLB) -- ISBN 0-7787-0123-9 (pbk.)
 1. Skateboarding--Juvenile literature. [1. Skateboarding.]
I. Rouse, Bonna, ill. II. Series.
  GV859.8 .C76 2002
  796.22--dc21
                                                      LC 2002002273

Contents

Wh t is skateboa, ding?

Skateboarding, or "skating," is a sport that involves performing **tricks**, or moves, on a board that has four wheels. It is an **individual** sport, which means that skateboarders, or "skaters," perform alone. Most skaters get together with their friends to practice tricks for the fun of it. Some skaters enjoy competing. They enter skateboarding competitions to display their talents and compare them with those of other skaters.

Competitions

For competitions, skaters put together a series of tricks called a **routine** or **run**. Judges award points for the difficulty of the tricks and the variety of tricks performed. Skaters lose points for falling off their boards. In most competitions, skaters attempt both **streetstyle** and **vertical** skating.

On the street

Streetstyle skating is exactly what it sounds like—skating as it is done on the street. It involves using streetside obstacles, such as curbs or benches, to perform tricks. Streetstyle can also be as simple as performing flips and jumps on a street.

Going up

Vertical skating is named for the position in which it puts skaters—moving straight up! Skaters use huge **ramps** to build speed, rolling from one side of the ramp to the other. They then leap above the **coping**, or edge of the ramp, and perform tricks in the air.

Slim beginnings

Skateboards made in the 1950s and 1960s were very narrow and were built for speed, not tricks. Most competitions were races. In the late 1970s, boards became much wider. The new shape made the boards easier to handle, and people started doing tricks made up of flips, jumps, and spins. Today, skateboards are built tough, and they are designed for performing a limitless number of tricks.

The essentials

Before you can start skating, you will need a few key items. Of course, getting a skateboard is the first step! A skater's equipment also includes protective gear and appropriate clothing. Equipment should fit well and feel comfortable.

Helmet and pads

A helmet and elbow and knee pads help protect you from serious injuries. You should always wear them when skating. You can also wear gloves to protect your hands from scrapes.

Food and water

Don't forget to bring water and a snack. You'll sweat and lose a lot of energy as you skate, so it is important to replace what you've lost with a quick snack. Don't eat your snack too quickly, or you might get stomach cramps.

Shoes

Many companies make shoes especially for skateboarding. You can find them at almost any athletic shoe store or skate shop. The shoes are light and have grooved or waffled soles to grip the board. Your shoes should provide strong heel support.

Skateboarders wear loose clothing that feels comfortable and allows them to move easily.

The deck

The "board" of a skateboard is also known as the **deck**. It has a rectangular shape with rounded corners. Each end is angled up to make a **kicktail**. The kicktails help skaters perform tricks in either direction. Most decks are made of several **plies**, or layers, of wood. The most popular design is about 29 inches (74 cm) long and nine inches (23 cm) wide.

Grip tape

Grip tape is placed on the deck to keep shoes from slipping off the skateboard. The sticky side attaches to the deck. The rough side, which is like sandpaper, "grips" the soles of your shoes.

tail

grip tape

kicktails

nose

deck

truck

Nice wheels

Bearings are small metal balls inside the wheel that allow it to spin smoothly. Double-shielded bearings are the most reliable and durable. Even the best bearings will rust, however, so avoid skating in the rain.

rail

wheel

Trucks

The wheel supports are called **trucks**. Each wheel is attached to its truck by a nut. Adjust the nut so that the wheel does not shift from side to side but can still spin freely.

Warming up

Stretching might sound like a weird thing to do before an afternoon skate, but it is a good idea! Warming up your muscles prevents painful sprains and strains that keep you on your couch and off your board! Take five minutes to perform these simple stretches, and you are on your way.

Quadriceps stretch

Stand on your left foot and use your left hand to support yourself against a wall. Bring your right foot up behind you until you can grab it with your right hand. Pull gently until you feel the stretch in the front of your leg. Hold the stretch for a count of ten and then stretch your left leg.

Leg lunges

Stand with your feet wide apart. Bend your left knee until you feel a stretch on the inside of your right leg. Hold the stretch for a count of five. Straighten up and switch sides.

Neck stretch

It is easy to hurt your neck, so do this stretch carefully. Tilt your head forward so that your chin points at your chest. Now slowly move your head toward one shoulder and then the other. Do not roll your head farther than feels comfortable and never roll your head backward.

Ankle stretch

Sit on the ground with one leg straight. Bend your other leg so that you can grab your foot. Gently move it in circles. When you have done ten circles, do ten more in the other direction. Change legs!

Arm circles

Swing your arms in large circles. Make the circles smaller and smaller until your arms are moving in tiny circles straight out to the side. Reverse the direction, starting with small circles and ending with giant ones.

9

Getting started

Once you have the proper equipment, you can start moving on your board. The key is to take things slowly. Don't feel frustrated if you can't do incredible tricks after only a few weeks! First you need to learn how to move and balance on your board.

> **Note:** Skateboards can be difficult to control. They often fly out from under skaters. Always skate in areas that are free of traffic and pedestrians.

Pushing off

To move, skaters put one foot on the ground and push the board forward. This action is called **pushing off**.

1. Place one foot on your board over the front truck, with your toes facing forward. Put your other foot on the ground next to the board.

2. Bend your knees slightly and push back with the foot on the ground. Lift it up, shift your weight to the foot on the board, and try to keep your balance.

3. Bring your foot forward and push it against the ground again. Pushing off repeatedly helps you gain speed.

Gliding

When you have built up enough speed you can **glide**, or coast along without pushing off. To get into a gliding position, turn your front foot slightly so that its outside edge faces forward. At the same time, lift your pushing foot onto the board and place it just behind the rear truck. Keep your arms outstretched for extra balance if you need it.

Getting goofy

Right-handed people tend to skate with their left foot on the front of the board. They use their right foot for pushing off and using the rear kicktail. Left-handed skaters often put their right foot forward on the board. This position is called **goofy foot**. When you are first starting out or trying new tricks, use the forward foot that feels most comfortable. When you get more experience, you can learn to skate **switchstance**, or with your other foot forward. Then you can do tricks in any direction.

Say what?

Skaters often talk about the **frontside** and **backside**. Frontside describes the side of the board your chest faces. If you normally put your right foot on the rear kicktail, the right side is your frontside. The backside is the left, or the side your back faces. Here are some other terms:

Frontside turn: If your right foot is on the tail, you are making a turn to the left. It is called a "frontside" turn because your chest faces outward as you turn.

Backside turn: If your right foot is on the tail, you are making a turn to the right.

Frontside hand: This hand is over the tail of the board.

Backside hand: This hand is over the nose of the board.

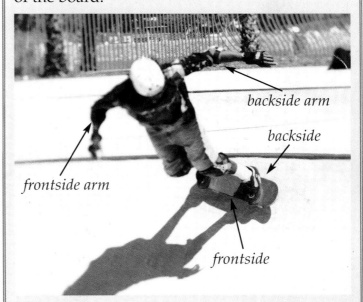

backside arm

backside

frontside arm

frontside

If you are more comfortable with your left foot at the tail, the directions will be opposite. For example, a backside turn will go to the left.

Stop it!

Once you get moving, you need to know how to stop! There are several ways to stop, including dragging one of your feet along the ground or even stepping off the board completely. The most precise stops are the **wheelie stop** and the **skidding stop**.

Slam it down

Wheelie stops are done by slamming down the tail of the board so it drags along the ground until the board stops. To do one, shift your rear foot to the deck's tail and push down. Use your arms to balance your body as the board drags along the ground. Keep your weight centered over the tail of the board.

Halt!

The skidding stop is more difficult than the wheelie, but it is also quicker. For this stop, quickly twist the board sideways so that the wheels skid along the ground. To do it, turn your whole body so that your chest is facing in the direction in which you are moving. As you turn, push down on the board so it turns with you. Keep your upper body leaning back and use your arms for balance.

Although the wheelie stop wears down your tail, it is the most common and useful way of stopping.

Don't use the skidding stop when traveling very fast—it is so sudden that you will be thrown forward and off your board.

Turning point

Trucks not only support your wheels—
they also allow the board to turn.
When you lean to one side or the other,
the trucks slightly **pivot**, or turn with
your weight. They allow the board
to turn in the direction you are leaning.

Before you attempt to turn, stand on
your board as you would while gliding.
Lean forward. Now lean backward.
Do you feel the board tilting underneath
you? Do the trucks feel too tight or too
wobbly? If they do, you may need to
adjust them. Continue leaning back
and forth until you feel comfortable
and balanced on the board.

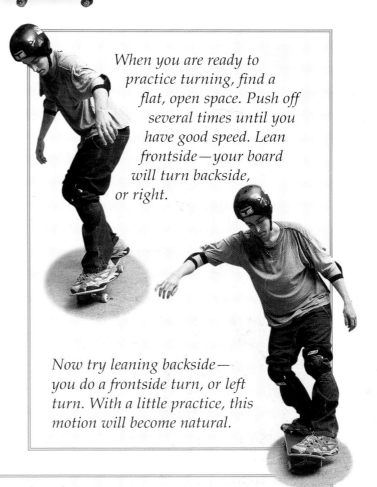

*When you are ready to
practice turning, find a
flat, open space. Push off
several times until you
have good speed. Lean
frontside—your board
will turn backside,
or right.*

*Now try leaning backside—
you do a frontside turn, or left
turn. With a little practice, this
motion will become natural.*

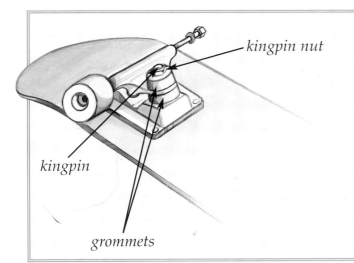

kingpin nut

kingpin

grommets

Adjusting your trucks

Every truck pivots around a center bolt
known as the **kingpin**. The kingpin has
two rubber washers called **grommets** that
protect the kingpin from wearing down.
There is a nut on the end of the kingpin
that pushes down on the grommets. If
your trucks feel too tight, use a wrench
to loosen each truck's kingpin nut a bit.
If the trucks are too loose, tighten the nut.

Kickturns

Leaning turns your board smoothly in a long, wide curve, but the turn requires a lot of room. **Kickturns** allow you to turn your board in a small space because they are sharp and quick. They can also be used instead of pushing off to move your board forward.

Twist and turn

A kickturn begins like a wheelie stop, but you do not push the tail down all the way. Instead, you lift up the nose of the board slightly, twist around in the direction you want to turn, and then lower the nose.

Kickturning

1. Start learning kickturns while simply standing on your board. Place your front foot over the front truck and your back foot on the kicktail.

2. Shift your weight back slightly and push down on the tail. Allow the nose to come up only a few inches. Begin turning the board by guiding the nose with your front foot. Twist your lower body at the waist along with the turn.

3. When the board is where you want it, shift your weight forward and push down the nose. Now try a kickturn moving the tail forward.

As your kickturning improves, push off and try kickturning while moving.

14

Moving with the kickturn

To move forward with kickturns, start from a **stationary**, or still, position. Perform a quick, short kickturn in one direction. As soon as the turn is finished, perform another kickturn in the opposite direction. Continue doing these turns back and forth, twisting at the waist as you go. You will find the board begins to move forward a bit at a time.

To do a manual, keep your weight centered over the rear truck and balance with your arms.

Consult the manual

In skateboarding, a **manual** is not a book—it's a trick. You do a manual by balancing on the rear wheels, without letting the kicktail touch the ground. It is fairly easy to do a manual after learning kickturns, but a **nose manual**, or balancing on the front wheels, takes a lot of practice. Learning to do manuals will help you gain better control over your board. Many professional skaters glide in manuals to add difficulty to their tricks.

In a nose manual, shift your front foot over the nose kicktail. Center your body over the front truck.

The ollie

The **ollie** is the basic building block of nearly all skating tricks. Doing an ollie is like jumping with your skateboard. You can use ollies to jump over or onto objects such as curbs, railings, and boxes. When you have mastered ollies, you can use them to start many other tricks (see page 22).

The ollie is a quick double motion that feels strange at first, but it is worth the effort. First you slam down the tail, and then you **level** out the board. The ollie uses moves that are similar to the kickturn, but they are quicker and more forceful. Foot placement, balance, and a strong jump are all important.

How to ollie

1. Ollies are difficult to do from a stationary position, so begin by pushing off a few times to get some speed. Now set up your feet. Place your front foot slightly behind the front truck and your back foot on the kicktail. Crouch down a bit, like a spring about to pop up.

2. Jump up and kick down! As you jump, snap the tail off the ground by putting more weight on your back foot. The board will come up with you.

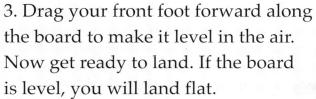

3. Drag your front foot forward along the board to make it level in the air. Now get ready to land. If the board is level, you will land flat.

Skateparks

Once you are comfortable with kickturns and ollies, you are ready to leave flat surfaces and take on some obstacles. A **skatepark** is the best place to find these challenges. It is free of cars and pedestrians. Many cities have indoor and outdoor skateparks full of impressive obstacles for maximum enjoyment.

Obstacles come in all shapes and sizes, but there are a few common types you should know. **Flat bars** are narrow, raised strips of metal. Skaters ollie to get on top of these obstacles and slide along them with their trucks or their deck. **Funboxes** are long wooden objects on which skaters jump and slide.

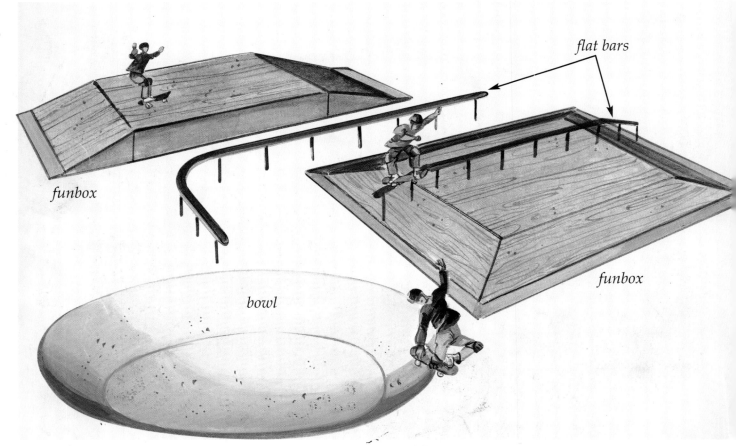

flat bars

funbox

funbox

bowl

Up and away

Skateparks also have many styles of ramps on which to skate. **Banks** are ramps with a gradual, even slope. These ramps help skaters **get air**, or leave the ground. **Quarter-pipe** and **half-pipe** ramps have very steep, curved slopes called **transitions**. Pipe ramps are great for gaining speed quickly. Skaters glide from side to side in a half-pipe ramp to build speed. They then perform tricks in the air on either side.

Have a bowl!

Bowls are similar to pipe ramps. They look just like giant bowls. Inside a bowl, skaters can go up in any direction they wish. They can also **carve**, or skate around the walls inside the bowl. Concrete pools are also used for skating—after the water is removed! Pools are similar to bowls, but they are often bigger and come in unusual shapes that offer skaters even more challenges.

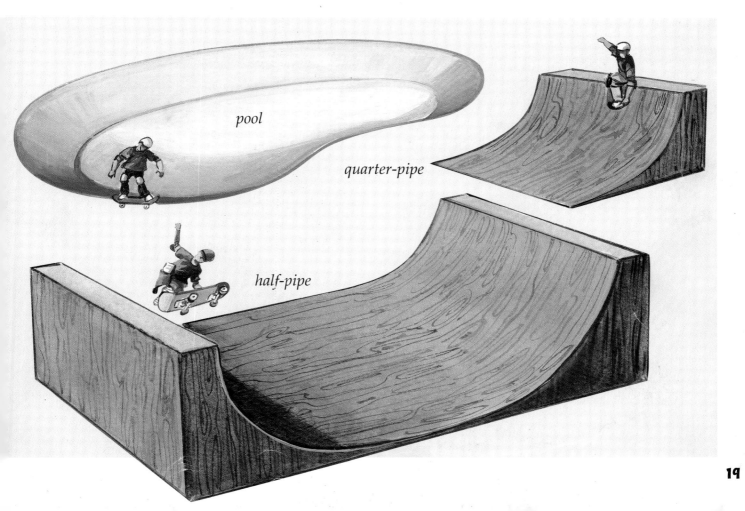

pool

quarter-pipe

half-pipe

Grinding and sliding

Grinding and **sliding** tricks are exactly what their names suggest. To grind, you drag your skateboard's metal trucks across an obstacle. To slide, you ride the board's deck along an obstacle. The obstacles are usually long, flat, and narrow objects such as bars, rails, and curbs. There are all kinds of grinds and slides. The tricks are usually named either for the part of the board that does the grinding or sliding, or for the obstacles on which they are performed. Before trying any of these tricks, make sure you are comfortable on your board and able to control it. You need a lot of speed to perform grinds and slides!

The 50-50 grind

The most common grind is the **50-50 grind**. You grind equally on both trucks—50 percent on the front truck and 50 percent on the rear truck. It's also called a **slappy grind**.

To 50-50 grind on a flat bar, head straight for the end of the bar. When you reach it, ollie onto it. Keep your eye on the obstacle. Adjust your feet in midair to move the board directly over the bar and grind on it.

You don't have to ollie for a 50-50 curb grind. Approach the curb at a bit of an angle. Just as you reach the curb, lean away to raise one side of your board. Then slam or "slap" your trucks against the curb and grind.

Nose grind

Approach the flat bar as you would for a 50-50 grind, but after ollieing in the air, lean forward onto your front foot. You should land on the bar with just your front truck. To **dismount**, do a **nollie**—while you're grinding, tap on the nose of the board and pop off the bar.

nose grind

nose grind from underneath

Nose slide

Approach alongside the flat bar and then ollie toward it. In the air, use your front foot to rotate the board and guide the nose onto the bar. Keep your weight balanced over your front foot as you slide. To dismount, lean down on the tail, twist your legs to rotate the board off the flat bar, and land.

Rail slide

A rail slide also starts with an ollie. You have to ollie high and far enough across the flat bar to get the center of your board over it. Your feet should be evenly spaced, with one foot over each truck. Your weight is directly over the board's center as the you slide along the bar or rail.

rail slide

rail slide from underneath

Flip tricks

Flip tricks are a big part of streetstyle skating. These tricks all begin the same way—with an ollie. Once the skater and board are in the air, however, the trick can go anywhere. The skater decides how to spin and flip the board in midair. The flip tricks below are a couple of common ones that will help you get started.

A kickflip

A pop-shove-it

Kickflip

This flip turns the board side-over-side under you. While skating, bring your feet toward the center of the board. Place the toes of your front foot under the backside rail of your deck. Jump up quickly and flip the board with your toes. When it turns upright again, place your feet back on the board to land and continue skating.

Pop-shove-it

This trick spins the board around in a half turn or a full turn. Start with an ollie. As you kick down with your back foot, sweep the back end of the board around to get it spinning. Put your feet back on the board and land when the spin is complete.

Dropping in

Tackling a skatepark's ramps and bowls is both exciting and scary. Before you worry about all the tricks you are going to do on the ramp, you need to learn how to **drop in**, or start at the coping and skate down the slope. This is not as easy as it sounds, so don't worry if you fall the first few times!

1. Wedge your rear truck against the coping. Place your weight on your rear foot on the kicktail. Put your front foot over the front truck but do not press down.

2. Lean forward and push down with your front foot. Crouch down and stay balanced over the board.

3. As you move down onto the ramp, come slightly out of the crouch.

On the ramp

After you drop in on the ramp, try the moves described here to help you get used to your new surroundings. They will challenge your balance, but they are easy to learn. Start with these simple tricks to improve your comfort and grace on the ramps. The really complex tricks can wait!

The fakie

A **fakie** is done by gliding up the ramp with normal footing and then sliding back down with the opposite foot leading. In other words, you glide back down without turning. Sounds simple? It is, but practicing fakies will improve your balance.

Kickturning on the ramp

Ramps change even the simplest skating moves—everything is different when it is done on an angle. When coming up the side of the ramp, try using a kickturn to come back down. The movements are the same as a kickturn on flat ground, but it takes a while to get used to the steep angle. Got that mastered? Then try this—a fakie down one side of the ramp and then a kickturn on the other side!

Rock 'n' roll

The **rock 'n' roll** is simple, but it looks impressive. Come straight up the ramp. Have your front foot on the nose kicktail. When you reach the coping, push down with your front foot. Balance the center of the board on the coping. Have your arms out for balance. Hold this position for a couple seconds. To **exit**, either kickturn and drop back onto the ramp, or step down on your tail and drop in with a fakie.

Grinding the coping

You can do grinds and slides on a ramp's coping. Imagine the coping as a curb, and you will be able to see how these tricks are done on it. You must balance a little differently than you do on a curb, however.

As you approach the top of the ramp, lean slightly backside to turn your board parallel to the coping. Your board will ride up onto the coping.

You can then perform a 50-50 grind along the edge. To dismount, give the tail a little kick and kickturn back down onto the ramp.

Getting some air

Vertical skating is all about getting your board in the air. **Aerial tricks**, or tricks performed in midair, are among the most difficult and exciting in skating. Once you are confident and balanced on the half-pipe, you are ready to get some air. The key to good air is speed. The faster you move on the ramp, the higher you can get.

Build up speed by going back and forth across a half-pipe or bowl. Crouch as you go down the ramp and stand up a bit as you come up on the other side. As you reach the top of the ramp, you can do a quick ollie to add to your air. You and your board will fly up and hang in the air for a moment before falling back onto the ramp.

Before doing any tricks, practice getting some air and landing safely on the ramp. Do not spin or flip—just concentrate on landing. You can try adding tricks later.

Spins

Spinning in midair is a big part of doing aerial tricks. Spins are often named for the **degrees** the board turns. For example, turning 360 degrees is a full spin or rotation. It is called a **360°**. A **180°**, or half rotation, is shown on the right. To spin, simply "throw" your body around after you leave the ramp. Keep one hand near the board to help guide it through the spin.

To do a backside 180°, this skater uses his frontside hand to hold the board through the spin.

He uses his backside hand for balance as he starts to land the aerial.

Plant your hand

Handplants combine grace and strength. They are one-handed handstands on or near the ramp's coping. A backside handplant is shown right.

As you reach the coping, lean down and plant your backside hand on the ramp. At the same time, grab the frontside of the board with your other hand. Throw your legs and the board up over your head and hold the position. Drop in by bringing your legs down and standing up.

Use your speed coming up the ramp to propel your legs into the air. Hold the plant as long as you can before dropping in.

Grab tricks

The number of **grab tricks** in skating is endless. These tricks are called grab tricks because the skater grabs the board with one or both hands while in the air. You can do grab tricks after an ollie on a flat surface, but the extra air that you get off a ramp makes these tricks easier to perform in a bowl or pipe.

*The **indy air** (top) and **melon air** (bottom) require flexibility, coordination, and quick movement.*

Basic grabs

The following grabs are good starting points. While airborne, grab the board with the proper hand—just let go before you hit the ground! Here are some examples:

Nose: Grab the nose of the deck with your backside hand.

Indy: Grab the frontside of the deck with your frontside hand.

Mute: Grab the frontside of the deck with your backside hand by reaching around your knee.

Melon: Grab the backside of the deck with your backside hand.

Complex grabs

So the basic grabs are too easy? Luckily, grabs can be as difficult as you can imagine. Complex grabs involve leg tucks, kicks, and even pulling the board out from under your body.

Tucking grabs

Japan air: Perform a mute grab (see page 28) while tucking your legs behind your body.

Rocket air: Use both hands to grab the nose of your board. At the same time, shift both feet to the kicktail. Blast off!

rocket air

Kicking grabs

Judo air: Grab the backside with your backside hand and kick your front foot forward. Return your foot to the board and land.

Frigid air: This grab is the same as a judo air, but you kick your front foot backward behind your body, instead of forward.

Airwalk: This grab is a nose grab with a double kick. Your back foot kicks **frigid**, or backward. Your front foot kicks **judo**, or forward.

judo air

finger-flip air

Pull away grabs

Cross air: Grab your board indy-style (see page 28) and pull it out from under your body. Straighten your legs and stretch out both arms so your body forms a cross. Then put the board back under your body and land. Very difficult!

Finger-flip air: Use a nose grab (see page 28) and pull your legs up off the board. Flip the board around once, place it under your legs, and land.

All together now!

The ultimate goal of learning tricks is to perform them in a series called a **combination**, or **combo**. In skating competitions, combos score big points. A combo can mean doing more than one trick while in the air. For example, a judo air performed while spinning your whole body around once would be a **360° judo air**.

Combos can also be done by stringing tricks together. Imagine this combo: ollie onto a flat bar and do a 50-50 grind along the bar. As you ollie off the bar, do a kickflip and land. This combo would be a **50-50 to kickflip**.

Great skaters are able to perform a grab trick followed by a kickflip—all before they land!

Bailing

There is one thing that never changes in skating—everybody falls, and they fall often. Even professionals! For this reason, pads and helmets are essential. You can also prevent injuries by knowing how to **bail**, or escape a failed trick. Bailing involves sliding or jumping away to safety.

A knee-slide bail

Bailing on a ramp

If you feel yourself losing balance on the edge of a ramp, you can use your knees to slide down the slope. Of course, this bail works best with knee pads! Simply fall to your knees and raise your arms to stay balanced as you slide down. Another simple ramp bail involves stepping off the board and side-stepping down the ramp. This method works best after failed tricks such as coping grinds.

A side-step bail down the ramp

Bailing from a flat bar

Falling onto a flat bar or stair railing after a failed grind or slide can really hurt! If you are losing control of the trick, jump to either side as far from the bar as you can.

Jumping clear of the flat bar

Glossary

backside Describing the side of the board that is behind you as you skate, or a turn in which your back faces outward

degree A unit used to measure circles; a circle is made up of 360 degrees

dismount To get off an obstacle

exit To finish a trick or get out of a skating position

frontside Describing the side of the board that is in front of you as you skate, or a turn in which your chest faces outward

kickturn A sharp turn made by kicking down the tail and pivoting the board on its back wheels

level To make the front and back ends of the board even while it is in midair

ollie A trick done by popping your skateboard up into the air

ramp A straight or curved slope that skaters ride up and down to set up and perform tricks

Note: Boldfaced words defined in the text may not appear in the glossary.

Index

1 2 3 4 5 6 7 8 9 0   Printed in the U.S.A.   1 0 9 8 7 6 5 4 3 2